WITCHES IN AMERICA

J. Elizabeth Mills

rosen publishing's
rosen central

NEW YORK

To Justi Grubor, thank you, my free-spirit friend!

Published in 2012 by The Rosen Publishing Group, Inc.
29 East 21st Street, New York, NY 10010

First Edition

Library of Congress Cataloging-in-Publication Data

Mills, J. Elizabeth.
Witches in America/J. Elizabeth Mills. — 1st ed.
    p. cm. —(America's supernatural secrets)
Includes bibliographical references and index.
ISBN 978-1-4488-5531-5 (library binding)—
ISBN 978-1-4488-5580-3 (pbk.)—
ISBN 978-1-4488-5581-0 (6-pack)
1. Witches—United States—History.
2. Witchcraft—United States—History. I. Title.
BF1573.M55 2012
133.4'30973–dc23

2011017989

Manufactured in the United States of America

CPSIA Compliance Information: Batch #W12YA: For further information, contact Rosen Publishing, New York, New York, at 1-800-237-9932.

Contents

Introduction

"When witches go riding, and black cats are seen, the moon laughs and whispers, 'tis near Halloween.'"
—Nineteenth-century Halloween postcard

Witches are a part of nearly every culture's folklore. Good witches and evil sorcerers, young enchantresses, and ancient crones have inspired literature, dance, artwork, movies, and dozens of other forms of creative expression. Pointy black hats and flying broomsticks, feline familiars, and wands are iconic representations of magic and spell-casting.

And yet witches have also instilled terror and loathing in a wide variety of societies. Why is this? What is it that people fear about witchcraft and magic? Historians believe that people prefer ordered societies, ones that are clearly defined with no uncertainty, no chaos. And government exists to preserve that order. Uncertainty and chaos are often regarded as evil and wasteful. Therefore, witchcraft, being wild and unpredictable, is a chaotic force and not to be trusted or tolerated.

A lack of knowledge and understanding about science, scientific principles, herbology, and medicine contributed to the mistrust and suspicion that swirled around the accused in Colonial Massachusetts, Connecticut, and Virginia. And a similar blind ignorance has manifested itself in other kinds of witch hunts throughout history. The internment of Japanese people during World War II; the McCarthy trials during the 1950's; the treatment and hurtful stereotyping of Muslims and Arabs in the years following September 11, 2001:

This woodcut illustration depicts a white witch and a black witch together with a devilish animal. It was believed that all forms of witchcraft were evil and had to be eradicated without distinction.

these are all instances where people relied on rumor and mass hysteria to guide their decisions about an ostracized group of people, rather than becoming informed and educated themselves.

Whether or not witchcraft and magic ultimately exist, our world does still contain unknown mysteries. It is imperative to keep an open mind to possibilities and developments, and look to the future for hope and inspiration. You never know what you might learn!

Chapter 1

Which Witch Is Which?

Say the word "witch" and you conjure up iconic images of tall, pointy black hats and long black dresses; a gnarled wand and a big black cauldron; and a spindly broom and a hissing black cat. Every Halloween, kids dash out of their homes ready to go trick-or-treating, many of them dressed head-to-toe like Hermione Granger or Harry Potter. Witches are ubiquitous, and they are fascinating to people of all ages. But what exactly is a witch?

Myths

The word "witch" comes from the old English word *wicca*. Another interpretation of the meaning is "practioner." "Wiccian" means to cast a spell, or bewitch someone. The term "witch" typically refers to someone, usually a woman, who practices magic or casts spells. And witchcraft is the craft practiced by a witch.

There are legends about witches in pretty much every culture, and each portrayal is unique. In some cases, the witches are good. They practice "white" or healing magic. In other cultures, witches are thought to perform evil spells and harm people with their black magic. Synonyms for "witch" include "sorceress," "magician," "mage," and "enchantress." Folk terms include "cunning," "wise," "hag," and "two-headed."

Witches were thought to participate in a nighttime ritual known as a witches' sabbath, in which they danced around in a circle in the middle of the forest with demons and devils.

Superstitions

A superstition is a belief about something or someone that is not based on fact, but upon rumor or popular opinion. One popular superstition is that if a black cat crosses your path, you will have bad luck. This isn't based on fact, but some people have had bad luck after seeing a black cat, and so the superstition was born.

People usually associate black cats with bad luck. During the middle ages, people often killed black cats, believing them to be evil omens.

Superstitions about witches have been around for centuries, certainly in the United States. Many of these unfounded beliefs centered on village women who possessed certain types of knowledge. Back in the 1600's, there were women who could tell which plants were harmful and which would soothe a burn. They could brew a tea that would make you calm or aid digestion, and they could dress a wound to help it heal by using crushed herbs. Other women were midwives. At a time when there were few doctors, midwives would tend to pregnant women and help them through the complicated procedure of childbirth. If all went well, it was thought that the women had used witchcraft to ensure a good outcome, and the "witch" was usually tolerated. If things went badly, however, and someone died, accusations of witchcraft flew fast and furious and resulted in bad trouble for the "witch."

Facts

People knew little about science, relying instead on biblical teachings to explain the world around them. If they witnessed something they didn't understand and couldn't explain with religion, they looked on it with suspicion. Furthermore, most people knew little about plants and even less about the human body. The women who did possess this knowledge were often mistrusted and believed to be witches who used magic to heal or harm the villagers.

Witches continue to practice today. There are people who practice all kinds of witchcraft, the most famous of which is Wicca, an earth-based pagan religion that focuses on nature and the cycle of the seasons. Far from the terrifying witches' sabbaths thought to be practiced by black-magic witches, Wicca is a "white" magic, its intent primarily to heal and connect with the world.

A Witch's Tools

It is believed that witches can tell the future, make potions that can cause people to fall in love or even die, fly, and even transform themselves into animals. So what do witches use to do their magic? The customary items include a broom, a wand, and a cauldron. But what are they used for? And why do we often see a black cat next to a witch?

Broom

While a witch's house is most likely not made out of gingerbread, there are certain items inside that are iconic and have important meaning. Possibly one

In this image, you can see a stereotypical depiction of a witch with all the usual accompaniments—pumpkin, cat, broom, cape, and hat—flying past a bright yellow harvest moon.

of the most recognizable items associated with a witch is a broom. Images of witches flying through the midnight sky on their broomsticks past a full harvest moon inspire excitement and dread in the young and the old. Brooms are obviously used for sweeping and cannot actually fly through the air. But some belief systems hold that the act of sweeping has magical significance and can summon or banish different kinds of energy over a threshold like a doorway. The idea of flying on a broomstick may have originated with the belief in a soul journey from the real world to the spirit world.

Cauldron

Moving into the house, there is a big, black pot hanging over a fire. Steam is curling out of the top. Once in a while, you can see a bubble or two pop. This is a cauldron, an old-fashioned iron pot used for cooking. Stereotypically, it can also be used for brewing potions and casting spells. In Shakespeare's play *Macbeth*, three witches recite a spell as they stand around a cauldron: "Double, double toil and trouble; fire burn and cauldron bubble." Eerie ingredients such as eye of newt and leg of toad or other unsavory items are thrown in and stirred with just the right spell to make something happen. The cauldron is found in many cultures around the world and is most often associated with the hearth—the cooking area in an old-time home, before kitchens and electric stoves. Cauldrons once hung in giant fireplaces by a curved handle on a hook, and flames would heat the bottom and sides to cook the contents.

Wand

On a table, you might find a long gnarled stick. A witch's wand is thought to direct magical energy and aid in casting spells. Wands may be made of all kinds of wood, and some witches believe the type of wood affects the out-come of the incantation. Wands may be plain or ornamented with stones and feathers. They may have carvings of letters and symbols, called runes, that aid in the practice of magic.

Fairy-tale Witches

Many fairy tales feature evil witches and dark enchantment. Two tales in particular feature particular kinds of witches. In "Sleeping Beauty," an evil fairy puts a spell on Sleeping Beauty so that when she turns eighteen, she will prick her finger on a spinning wheel and die. However, she only falls into a deep sleep, thanks to some quick-thinking good fairies. In "Snow White," Snow White is similarly bewitched, this time by an evil queen who has disguised herself as a hag. She convinces Snow White to eat a juicy red apple that's been poisoned so that the witch can once again be the fairest in the land. Like Sleeping Beauty, though, Snow White only falls asleep.

Book of Shadows

Also sitting on the table might be a Book of Shadows. Filled with handwritten notes, a Book of Shadows is a witch's reference and is unique to her craft. She writes her spells, experiments, and findings in it—a magical field notebook. Possession of any magical object was regarded with suspicion, however, and had to be kept hidden. Hence its name—women kept their books in the shadows to avoid detection.

Familiars

Curled up by the hearth is a sleek black cat. It was believed that witches had animal companions that assisted in casting spells and other magical duties. These animal partners had close bonds with their owners, and witches were thought to shape-shift into their familiars, as these animals were called, at will. The most common critters believed to be familiars included bats, toads, ravens, rats, and rabbits. Rumor had it that familiars possessed their own magical powers, making them even more dangerous.

What spell might this witch be brewing in her cauldron? Traditional images such as this one lead us to believe that all witches are hags, when this is not true.

Cats are the most iconic of all animals thought to be witches' familiars. Perhaps this is because cats are not fully understood. They are aloof, independent animals that don't seem to need humans in the way that dogs do. Whatever the reason, cats, especially black cats, represent magic for many cultures, including our own. A common Halloween image involves a black cat wearing a witch's hat, sitting near a cauldron. The concept of a familiar struck fear in early Americans, not to mention the possibility of shape-shifting. A woman who owned several cats and kept to herself was often viewed with suspicion and avoided. She did not fit in with the rest of the community, and so she was an outcast.

Chapter 2

Colonial Witches

In the bleak winter of 1692 in the Massachusetts Bay Colony, a frightening event took place that would forever haunt the settlement and its inhabitants. A group of girls began to accuse members of the colony of being witches. In the end, more than 150 people were accused, 20 people were hanged, several more died in prison, and one man was crushed to death. How did this happen?

Salem, Massachusetts, 1692

Long before the United States existed as a country, there were people called Puritans who traveled to America to escape religious persecution in England. They wanted to practice their own religion, a very strict form of Christianity, without any problems from the British government.

Puritans led severe lives. Not only was the environment in early America harsh and unforgiving, but also people worked long hours and allowed themselves few comforts. The Puritan community rewarded conformity—you were expected to fit in and do what everyone else did. Anyone who stood out or refused to follow the rules was frowned upon. For example, the clothing was simple and monochrome so as to avoid attention and vanity. The meetinghouse was the place of worship and the center of the Puritan community. And the main book in every home was the Bible, which dictated how people were to live and treat one another.

The church was the center of the Puritan community. Ministers used the Bible to dictate to their parishioners how to dress, how to behave, and what to believe.

Superstitions

Puritans feared God, but they feared the Devil just as much. They believed the Devil was real, and had the intent to influence and harm. This led to strongly held superstitions and a rampant and unyielding paranoia about magic, witches, and witchcraft—a practice thought to involve dealing with the Devil.

The main economy at the time was farming, so the settlers depended on harvests and livestock for sustenance. They toiled in rocky, unforgiving fields, attempting to sow seeds and make a living. If a cow fell ill, or a crop failed, it was believed that either it was God's will that these misfortunes had taken place or a neighbor had cursed the livestock or land. Puritans were highly suspicious of one another, especially over land disputes.

The Accusers

Winter nights in Salem were idle times, especially for children. In the upstanding Parris household, a West Indian slave named Tituba passed the long dark evenings telling fortunes and fantastical stories to two girls, Abigail Williams and Betsy Parris. These meetings were secret, though, because these activities were forbidden. Whether the guilt of these illicit meetings affected the girls, or whether it was something else, they began acting strangely. They shrieked and fell on the floor, shaking, and they complained that someone was pinching them. Reverend Parris asked them what was wrong. Afraid of being punished for disobedience, Abigail and Betsy accused Tituba of bewitching them. Tituba, equally afraid of retribution, immediately pleaded guilty to witchcraft and claimed there were other witches in the community. Thus began the wave of accusations.

The Accused

Sarah Good, a local homeless woman who was often seen begging for food and shelter, was the next to be accused. Sarah Osborne, who rarely attended worship meetings, was the third. These women were all outcasts or different in some way.

In the spring, a court was hastily set up, with John Hathorne and Jonathan Corwin presiding as local magistrates, to hear the accusations and decide what these women's fates should be. These trials became famous for their dramatic action. In the middle of the proceedings, the girls would stare off into space, declaring they were seeing a specter of the witch's familiar up in the rafters of the meetinghouse. They'd fall to the ground and shake, crying out for their "tormentor" to stop hurting them. They'd scream and utter words in incomprehensible speech. Only when the accused person was removed from the room or ordered to stay still would the "affliction" stop.

Tituba and the Children.

Tituba's unfamiliar accent and unusual traditions and stories fascinated and frightened the Parris children, resulting in lively winter evenings and exciting courtroom drama.

The Trial

The girls were the center of attention as well as the focus of fear in these trials. Their reactions to the presence of the accused were frightening and whipped the community into a great state of fear and suspicion. Accusations flew fast and furious, directed not just at outcasts but at well-regarded citizens, too, such as Martha Corey, who attended church regularly. Members of the community began to wonder who among them could be called a witch, if not even piety could keep one safe.

Bridget Bishop

In June, Governor William Phipps assembled a Special Court of Oyer (which means "to hear") and Terminer (which means "to decide") to hear these cases. The first person to be sentenced in this court was a woman named Bridget Bishop. Known for her unconventional clothing and independent mind, Bishop was regarded with suspicion in Salem. She spoke for herself, was married three times, and fought openly with her husbands. She also ran a tavern in her home, a practice her neighbors disliked. Furthermore, her tavern and lands were successful while others' were not, a further sore point in Salem. Though she claimed she was innocent on the charge of witchcraft, the girls' accusations were not questioned, and so Bishop became the first person to be hanged on a hill that would later be known as Gallows Hill. The sentencing and accusations continued. By the end of September 1692, the jails were full and twenty people had been hanged.

Spectral Evidence

Increase Mather, a respected minister at the time and president of Harvard College, had written extensively on the subject of witchcraft and objected to the use of what he called "spectral evidence" in the Court of Oyer and Terminer. This term referred to testimony about dreams and visions by the girls

Increase Mather, father of Cotton Mather, stood against the witchcraft tests that included reciting the Lord's Prayer, floating, or possessing black marks on the body.

used to convict the accused. He felt that this kind of evidence was not trustworthy and feared that innocent people might be put to death. In a line that would become famous, he said, "It were better that ten suspected witches should escape than that one innocent person should be condemned." He brought his concerns to the governor, who decreed that no further arrests for witchcraft would be allowed. He decided to dismantle the court in October. And he released those who remained in the jails.

Why Did the Witch Hunt Happen?

It is not known what exactly set off the spark that led to this tragedy. Most likely, it was a number of factors. Salem Village and Salem Town, nearby communities, were battling over property disputes. It may be that some of the accused were involved in these disputes. Salem Village, a poorer settlement with mostly farmers, also felt excluded and oppressed by the wealthier inhabitants of Salem Town. In addition, Salem Village had its own division between the tradesmen who lived near Ipswich Road, the commerce road, and the farmers who lived farther away and shunned prosperity as a sin. Many of the people who were accused of witchcraft lived near Ipswich Road, and those who did the accusing lived on the farms of Salem Village.

The Aftermath

Eventually, all who had been in prison were pardoned by May 1693. And after the trials were over, many of the people who took part in these proceedings, including a judge, publicly stated that they had been wrong and felt bad about what had happened. On January 14, 1697, the colony held a day of fasting and reflection on the tragedy of Salem, Massachusetts. In 1702, a

A Modest Enquiry

Into the Nature of

Witchcraft,

AND

How Persons Guilty of that Crime may be *Convicted* : And the means used for their Discovery Discussed, both *Negatively* and *Affirmatively*, according to SCRIPTURE and EXPERIENCE.

By John Hale,

Pastor of the Church of Christ in *Beverley*, *Anno Domini* 1697.

When they say unto you, seek unto them that have Familiar Spirits and unto Wizzards, that peep, &c To the Law and to the Testimony; if they speak not according to this word, it is because there is no light in them, Isaiah VIII. 19, 20.
That which I see not teach thou me, Job 34 32.

BOSTON in N. E.
Printed by *B. Green,* and *J. Allen,* for *Benjamin Eliot* under the Town House. 1702

Reverend John Hale initially supported the Salem witch trials and then later changed his mind, publishing a book called *A Modest Enquiry into the Nature of Witchcraft*, in which he critiqued the proceedings.

general court declared that the trials had been unlawful. Nine years later, the Massachusetts colony passed a bill that returned to the accused their good names and all their rights, including restitution of 600 pounds to their descendants. A formal apology from the state of Massachusetts, however, did not come until 1957, nearly three hundred years after the trials. One sad anecdote: the bodies of those who were hanged were not allowed to be buried in consecrated ground, such as a church cemetery, because of the nature of their alleged crime. Though it is not known exactly what happened to them, it is believed that the families claimed their loved ones and buried their bodies elsewhere. There is a memorial today in Salem to honor the victims of the witch trials.

Chapter 3

More Witch Trials and Tales

The Salem witch trials are most likely the best-known witchcraft-related event in American history. But this country has had a long and involved past involving false accusations and unfounded executions that predate Salem and continue long after.

Connecticut

About fifty years before the Salem trials, Connecticut was already experiencing witch hysteria. A fearful belief in the forces of evil, witchcraft, enchantment, and the dark arts, a fear that was fueled by European persecutions and strict religious practices, was common in Puritan times. Colonists also faced violent conflicts with American Indians over land, epidemics, natural disasters, uncertainty about the government, and other difficult events. Times were hard, and people needed a scapegoat on which to focus their frustrations, someone to hold responsible for their difficulties.

Hartford Witch Panic

The first known North American witchcraft trial and execution took place in Connecticut in 1647. The victim was Alice Young. In the years between

During the time of the trials, settlers had land disputes with Native Americans over territory rights. The settlers often took land that didn't belong to them, without regard for those who lived there first.

1648 and 1663, when the final execution in Hartford took place, thirty-four people were put on trial, and nearly half of them were convicted and hanged. Magistrates were fervent in their zeal to accuse and eliminate all witches, a zeal they would find again in Salem in 1692. However, in 1655, Governor John Winthrop, the son of the governor of Massachusetts and one of the most popular doctors in New England, intervened in the trials, decreeing that accused witches were not to be executed. He had an interesting insight into witchcraft, as he was familiar with forms of earth-based magic such as astrology and alchemy. He knew how difficult it was to perform any kind of real magic, and so certainly such a large number of people could not possibly be actual witches. Though the executions started up again while he was in England in 1661, upon his return Winthrop fought for the end of this mass hysteria. Little by little, the magistrates were convinced to act more reasonably and look at the evidence before them with moderation and objectivity. Conviction could no longer rely on only one witness's testimony of a supernatural event. Two people had to witness it at the same time. Since this was rarely if ever the case, testimonies were thrown out. Thus, New England entered a quiet period, from 1663 to 1688, in which there were no executions and few, if any, accusations.

Virginia

Early Americans devised tests to find out if an accused person was a witch or not. One of the most recognizable was the water test. The accused's hands and feet were bound and her body dropped into a deep body of water. If she were innocent and pure, God's water would accept her and she would sink. Few people in early America knew how to swim. So not only would the accused drown, but her neighbors would have no way to pull her out. If, however, she were a witch, the water would reject her and she would float. In this case, though she had survived the water test, she would be hung on the gallows for the crime of witchcraft.

A Witch Bottle

The interesting thing about the witch trials is that no actual witches were ever found. Only innocent people were accused, jailed, and hanged. However, it seems there may be an artifact of "white witchcraft," discovered during excavations at Governor Printz State Park in Essington, Pennsylvania. The object is a glass bottle with six round-headed pins inside and sealed with a wooden plug. It seems no other bottle with such contents has yet been found in the United States. Its construction and upside-down burial appear connected with an English charm to ward off witchcraft-related pain and was most likely put underground in the mid-1700's. This was a common practice in colonial America.

Grace Sherwood

The year 2006 marked the three hundredth anniversary of the last witch trial in America. In 1706, in Virgina, a forty-six-year-old woman named Grace Sherwood was charged with the practice of witchcraft. Witnesses accused the midwife, widow, healer, and mother of cursing crops, causing the death of livestock, harming her patients, and other acts. To prove her innocence or guilt, she was "ducked" in the Lynnhaven River, which was deemed to be "consecrated" water—water blessed by God. Bound and weighted down by a Bible, she was thrown from a boat into the water at an area now known as Witchduck Point. She managed to undo her bindings and float up to the surface, whereupon she was immediately charged as a witch and sent to jail for seven years. After her release, Sherwood returned home and lived with her family until she died, at age eighty. However, her name was not cleared until July 10, 2006, in a formal document signed by Virginia Governor Tim Kaine.

Grace Sherwood suffered through a ducking test and a long jail term, all based on rumors of witchcraft. Today, her statue serves as a reminder to stand up for those who have been wrongly accused.

Tennessee

Many years later, a haunting believed to be witnessed and documented by hundreds of people, among them future president Andrew Jackson, represents one of the most famous instances of paranormal events in history. The events are alleged to have taken place between 1817 and 1821.

The Bell Witch Cave is located in an isolated area of Adams, Tennessee, near a farm owned by the Bell family. Some believe that when the witch finally left the house, she fled to the cave for safety. Otherwise, the cave is not directly involved with the haunting.

Bell Witch

In 1804, the Bell family moved to a 320-acre (129-hectare) farm in Tennessee along the Red River. The family belonged to the local church and was active within the community. Their lives were uneventful until 1817, when strange things began to happen. One day, John Bell found a beast on his farm that seemed unnatural. He described it as having the body of a dog and the head of a rabbit. Not sure what else to do, he shot the animal and it vanished. He put the incident out of his mind, until his children complained of hearing rats gnawing on their bed and making noises around the house. But Bell could not find a source for the noises. During several frightening encounters with the unseen terror, his daughter, Betsy, allegedly experienced hair pulling and assaults. She developed marks on her body as though something was whipping her, but there was no one there. Bedclothes were tossed around, pulled away from the children during the night. Whispering voices added to the growing hysteria in the family. Unnerved, the Bell family did their best to hide these strange occurrences and keep everything a secret over the next year. But then the neighbors came and stayed at the house and experienced the terrifying events. They told John Bell to let out his secret and have people come investigate. But this only seemed to make the spirit grow stronger, according to the legend.

3C 38

BELL WITCH

To the north was the farm of John Bell, an early, prominent settler from North Carolina. According to legend, his family was harried during the early 19th century by the famous Bell Witch. She kept the household in turmoil, assaulted Bell, and drove off Betsy Bell's suitor. Even Andrew Jackson who came to investigate, retreated to Nashville after his coach wheels stopped mysteriously. Many visitors to the house saw the furniture crash about them and heard her shriek, sing, and curse.

TENNESSEE HISTORICAL COMMISSION

The Bell Witch Cave has been an attraction for ghost hunters for decades, and the events surrounding the Bell Witch have become a part of Tennessee folklore and legend.

In some records, the spirit could speak and communicate with people. Its name was Kate, and it had only one mission: to kill John Bell and stop the marriage between his daughter and a local boy. Bell died in 1820 of an apparent poisoning, and Betsy ended the engagement. The circumstances surrounding Bell's death were very mysterious.

But who is the Bell Witch? It is believed that she was Kate Batts, a neighbor of the Bell family, who thought Bell had cheated her in a purchase of land and, upon suing him, vowed to haunt him and his descendants. Though the house has been torn down, many believe the spirit still haunts the land. And the mystery of the two-hundred-year-old Bell Witch has never been solved.

Chapter 4

Witches in Popular Culture

Witches are an integral part of our cultural heritage. In every form of cultural expression, there has been a reference to or a focus on witchcraft and its practitioners. How have these cultural references helped shape your view on witches?

Literature

From Nathaniel Hawthorne's *The House of Seven Gables* to *The Crucible* by Arthur Miller, to more contemporary works of literature, authors have taken on the subjects of witches and witch trials with purpose and imagination. Miller based his play on the Salem witch trials, but he was also commenting on the McCarthy trials of the 1950's and the panic that ensued there, showing the similarity to colonial Massachusetts. Shakespeare wrote about the rise of the king of Scotland and drew upon the hysteria in England over witches and sorcery to portray the three Weird Sisters in *Macbeth*. Witches have played a part in literature for centuries.

Chronicles of Narnia

C. S. Lewis's Narnia series has been read and interpreted in dozens of ways since its publication in the mid-1900's. Its simple themes of good and evil and

Three witches lead Macbeth to believe he will become king, in Shakespeare's famous play *Macbeth*. In fact, the play opens with the three witches brewing a potion during a storm.

honor and betrayal ring true with children across the generations. And perhaps one of its most famous characters, next to the lion, Aslan, is the White Witch. In the first book, *The Lion, the Witch, and the Wardrobe*, Edmund encounters her in the magical land of Narnia. She appears very friendly and affable to him, offering treats and a seat on her sleigh. She asks only that he bring his brother and two sisters to visit her—the sons of Adam and daughters of Eve, as she puts it. Lucy, the youngest in the Pevensie family, has other thoughts about the witch, based on her experiences with another Narnian citizen, Mr. Tumnus, a faun. He says the White Witch is evil—she has spies and she makes it always winter and never Christmas. The story thus unfolds as a battle between the dark forces of the witch and Aslan's army of good—a classically negative view of witches and witchcraft.

Philip Pullman's series His Dark Materials features witches with daemons—spirits that take animal form, similar to familiars. The Finnish witch queen Serafina Pekkala, played here by Eva Green, has a large grey goose for a daemon.

His Dark Materials

Philip Pullman, on the other hand, chose to portray witches as friends and allies to humans. In fact, his view of good and evil are quite different from those of other contemporary fantasy series. In his books, people's souls exist outside their bodies in the form of animals called daemons. And the world is run by an authoritative religious group known as the Magisterium. In *The Golden Compass*, the opening book in his series His Dark Materials, a witch queen named Serafina Pekkala warns of a place called Bolvanger, where children are being cut away from their daemons so that they will never experience sin. Serafina offers to help Lyra, the main character, in her quest to save the other children and take on the Magisterium's terrible plan. Witches live a very long time in Pullman's world, and so they do not have many human companions. They fly on branches of a tree called Cloud-Pine and believe that they could not live without flight. Serafina's daemon is a grey goose named Kaisa.

Harry Potter

The Harry Potter series perhaps best illustrates and redefines the classic stereotypes of witches and witchcraft covered in this book. Witches exist in our world, but in secret, with an entire government office designated for that very purpose. There is a magical academy, called Hogwarts, where young wizards and witches learn how to access and wield their magical powers, as well as learn the basics of herbology, potions, and divination—classes that hearken back to the stereotypical practices of witches, which prove to be very handy when combating the forces of evil. There is a great emphasis in this series on portraying the world of Harry Potter as normal and parallel to our own, with a few differences here and there.

As Harry is preparing for his first year, he purchases a cauldron, an owl (similar to a familiar), black robes, a pointed hat, magical books, and several other things that are typically associated with the practice of magic. But it is

Voldemort, played here by Ralph Fiennes, is one of the most powerful evil wizards in children's literature. His followers bear special marks on their arms that they use to call the Dark Lord.

his purchase of a wand that is highlighted in this world. Wands are obtained at a shop called Ollivanders, whose proprietor utters the ominous words, "It's really the wand that chooses the wizard, of course." And the wand that chooses Harry turns out to be the twin of the wand carried by Harry's nemesis, the dark lord Voldemort. For in Harry's world, though wizards and witches are portrayed favorably, there are also bad wizards who do nasty, evil things with magic. Voldemort's followers, known as Death Eaters, are marked by a symbol on their wrists, similar to the mark that witches in Puritan times were believed to have. Good and evil are given equal play in the series, and both appeal to Harry at different times in his life at Hogwarts. On the lighter side, there is a wizarding form of soccer, called Quidditch, that's played dozens of feet in the air on broomsticks. And Professor McGonagall, as well as other adults in the book, are shape-shifters.

Television

Television brought a new visual element to the iconic witch. In series such as *Bewitched* and *Sabrina, the Teenage Witch*, attractive women are portrayed as witches, rather than the old hags in fairy tales. Spells are used for good purposes, even household activities, making them ubiquitous and mundane, rather than supernatural and frightening.

Merlin

This relatively new series on the SyFy channel focuses on the legend of the famous wizard and adviser to King Arthur. Merlin and Arthur are portrayed as young men—Merlin fights to master his magical powers in the face of a kingdom intolerant of the use of magic, and Arthur tries to find his way under the scrutiny of his father, Uther Pendragon. Magic is once again kept hidden and secret, but it is intrinsic and essential to the future ascension of Arthur to the throne of Camelot. As with Harry Potter, the focus is more on wizards than witches.

The Rest of the Story

There is another side to the story of the Wicked Witch of the West, thanks to a book called *Wicked: The Life and Times of the Wicked Witch of the West*, by Gregory Maguire, which was made into a musical called simply *Wicked*. Elphaba is a young witch with green skin who is friends with a cheerful blond witch named Glinda. Themes of alienation, bullying, and intolerance run through the story and echo the persecutions suffered by accused witches throughout history.

Movies

With longer running times and captive audiences, movies have an even greater power than television to influence how we view magic and witchcraft. Feature-length reimaginings of books, as well as original screenplays, transport viewers to all kinds of enchanted locations: Mordor and the Shire in *The Lord of the Rings*, the island of Tortuga in *Pirates of the Caribbean*, and France in Disney's animated *Beauty and the Beast*.

The Wizard of Oz

The Emerald City is the destination in this 1939 movie, a beloved classic for generations since. A stunning retelling of the favorite book, this movie performs an interesting trick of foreshadowing by casting Margaret Hamilton as both Almira Gulch, the nasty neighbor in Kansas who is bitten by Toto and tries to take him away, and the Wicked Witch of the West in Oz. Here we can see the familiar touchstones—pointy hat, green skin, mean disposition, and flying broomstick (that is mirrored in the bicycle Gulch rides during the tornado).

Complete with black hat, black dress, crooked nose, and long fingernails, the
Wicked Witch of the West inspires fear in everyone, especially Dorothy and her
friends, the Cowardly Scarecrow, the Lion, and the Tin Man, in *The Wizard of Oz*.

The Little Mermaid

Did you know that witches existed under the sea, too? In this retelling of the Hans Christian Andersen fairy tale, a young mermaid named Ariel longs to be human and meet the prince she rescues one day in the ocean. She wants to grow legs and feet and walk on land more than anything else in the world. So she goes to see Ursula, the sea witch. Ursula is understanding and sympathetic and ready to help, but she has one requirement for payment—Ariel's beautiful singing voice. Ursula is old and plump and has a low, gravelly voice. She wants to be young and pretty once again, with a voice to match. When the transaction is made, Ursula reveals the final catch—Ariel will turn back into a mermaid unless she can convince the prince to fall in love with her. But she no longer has a voice! Ursula, like the Wicked Witch, is portrayed as an evil being, selfish, vindictive, and jealous—stereotypically a witch.

Glossary

alchemy A medieval chemical science that aims to transform base metals into gold.

astrology The study of stars in terms of how they influence human life and behavior.

cauldron A big black pot used for cooking or brewing potions.

charm The chanting or reciting of a magic spell.

familiar An animal, often a cat, that is believe to assist witches in their magic.

midwife A person who assists women in childbirth.

pagan A follower of a religion that believes in many gods.

puritan A member of a sixteenth- and seventeenth-century Protestant group in England and New England that opposed ceremonial worship and practiced a more rigorous moral code.

rune A written character believed to have magical significance.

spell A spoken enchantment.

superstition A belief or practice resulting from ignorance, fear of the unknown, or trust in magic or chance.

Wicca A religion influenced by pre-Christian beliefs and practices of western Europe that affirms the existence of supernatural power and that emphasizes ritual observance of seasonal and life cycles.

witch A person who practices magic, often black magic, with the aid of a devil or familiar.

witchcraft The use of sorcery or magic.

For More Information

Bell Witch Cave
430 Keysburg Road
Adams, TN 37010
(615) 696-3055
Web site: http://www.bellwitchcave.com
Visit the historic Bell Witch Cave and learn the details of one of the most
    famous mysteries in American history.

Canadian Museum of Civilization
100 Laurier Street
Gatineau, QC K1A 0M8
Canada
(819) 776-7000
Web site: http://www.civilization.ca.
This museum features exhibits on Canada's First Peoples and government sys-
    tems, such as the post office, and has a children's museum and more.

The Jonathan Corwin House/ The Witch House
310 ½ Essex Street
Salem, MA 01970
(978) 744-8815
Web site: http://www.salemweb.com/witchhouse
The Witch House, home of Judge Jonathan Corwin, is the only structure still
    standing in Salem with direct ties to the witchcraft trials of 1692.

McCord Museum of Canadian History
690 Sherbrooke West

Montreal,QC H3A 1E9
Canada
(514) 398-7100
Web site: http://www.mccord-museum.qc.ca/
The museum aims to shed light on the history and culture of Canada and
    bring its people together.

Salem Witch Museum
Washington Square North
Salem, MA 01970
(978) 744-1692
Web site: http://www.salemwitchmuseum.com
The Salem Witch Museum brings you back to the Salem of 1692 with a
    dramatic history lesson using stage sets with life-size figures, dramatic
    lighting, and a narrative overview of the witch trials.

The Witch's Hut
Mezz. Unit 58-81 Garry Street
Winnipeg, MB R3C 4J9
Canada
(204) 989-8300
Web site: http://www.gccmb.com
The Witch's Hut is a major cultural attraction in the city and brings to life the
    story of "Hansel and Gretel."

Web Sites

Due to the changing nature of Internet links, Rosen Publishing has developed
an online list of Web sites related to the subject of this book. This site is
updated regularly. Please use this link to access the list:

http://www.rosenlinks.com/amss/wtch

For Further Reading

Dahl, Roald. *The Witches*. London, England: Jonathan Cape, 1983.

Davis, Amy M. *Good Girls and Wicked Witches: Women in Disney's Feature Animation*. Eastleigh, England: John Libbey Publishing, 2006.

Ehrenreich, Barbara. *Witches, Midwives & Nurses: A History of Women Healers*. New York, NY: Feminist Press, 2010.

Goss, K. David. *The Salem Witch Trials: A Reference Guide*. Westport, CT: Greenwood Press, 2008.

Guiley, Rosemary Ellen. *The Encyclopedia of Witches, Witchcraft, and Wicca*. New York, NY: Checkmark Books, 2008.

Ingram, Martin Van Buren. *An Authenticated History of the Famous Bell Witch*. Rockville, MD: Wildside Press, 2009.

Konigsburg, E. L. *Jennifer, Hecate, Macbeth and Me*. New York, NY: Aladdin, 1967.

Parks, Peggy J. *Witches*. San Diego, CA: ReferencePoint Press, 2008.

Pipe, Jim. *You Wouldn't Want to Be a Salem Witch! Bizarre Accusations You'd Rather Not Face*. Brighton, England: Salaryia, 2009.

Pullman, Philip. *The Golden Compass*. New York, NY: Knopf, 1995.

Raedisch, Linda. *Night of the Witches: Folklore, Traditions, & Recipes for Celebrating Walpurgis Night*. Woodbury, MN: Llewellyn, 2011.

Rowling, J. K. *Harry Potter and the Sorceror's Stone*. London, England: Bloomsbury, 1997.

Speare, Elizabeth George. *Witch of Blackbird Pond*. Boston, MA: Houghton Mifflin, 1958.

The Witches' Almanac: Spring 2010–Spring 2011. Providence, RI: Witches Almanac, 2009.

Bibliography

Becker, Marshall J. "An American Witch Bottle." Archaeological Institute of America. Retrieved February 11, 201(http://www.archaeology.org/online/features/halloween/witch_bottle.html. 2009).

Illes, Judika. *The Weiser Field Guide to Witches: From Hexes to Hermione Granger, from Salem to the Land of Oz.* San Francisco, CA: Red Wheel/Weiser, 2010.

McDougald-Williams, Erin. "America's Most Haunted Location: Bell Witch Cave." Suite101.com., August 31, 2010. Retrieved February 11, 2011 (http://www.suite101.com/content/americas-most-haunted-location-bell-witch-cave-a280783).

Meltzer, Milton. *Witches and Witch-hunts: A History of Persecution.* New York, NY: The Blue Sky Press, 1999.

Murphy-Hiscock, Arin. *The Way of the Hedge Witch: Rituals and Spells for Hearth and Home.* Avon, MA: Adams Media, 2009.

Mysteries of the Unexplained Blog. November 21, 2010. Retrieved February 11, 2011 (http://mysteriesoftheunexplainedblog.blogspot.com/2010/11/bell-witch-cave-adams-tennessee.html).

Myths Encyclopedia: Myths and Legends of the World. "Witches and Wizards." Retrieved February 11, 2011 (http://www.mythencyclopedia.com/Wa-Z/Witches-and-Wizards.html).

Official Home of the Historic Bell Witch Cave. "An American Haunting." Retrieved February 11, 2011 (http://www.bellwitchcave.com).

Salem Witch Museum. Retrieved February 11, 2011 (www.salemwitchmuseum.com).

Stark, Bruce P. "Witchcraft in Connecticut." Connecticut's Heritage Gateway. Retrieved February 11, 2011 (http://www.ctheritage.org/encyclopedia/ctto1763/witchcraft.htm).

Virginia Historical Society. "The 'Witch of Pungo': 300 Years After Her Conviction, Governor Restores Grace Sherwood's Good Name." Retrieved February 11, 2011(http://www.vahistorical.org/news/gracesherwood.htm).

Wagner, Stephen. "The Bell Witch." About.com. Retrieved February 11, 2011 (http://paranormal.about.com/od/trueghoststories/a/aa041706.htm).

Welcome to Salem, Massachusetts: The City Guide. "The Salem Witch Trials." Retrieved February 11, 2011 (www.salemweb.com/guide/witches/shtml).

Woodward, Walter P. "New England's Other Witch-hunt: The Hartford Witch-hunt of the 1660s and Changing Patterns in Witchcraft Prosecution." Organization of American Historians Magazine of History. Retrieved February 11, 2011 (http://maghis.oxfordjournals.org/content/17/4/16.ful).

Index

B

Bell Witch, 29–31
Bishop, Bridget, 19
Book of Shadows, 12
brooms, 4, 6, 10–11, 38

C

cats, 4, 6, 8, 12, 14
cauldrons, 6, 10, 11
Chronicles of Narnia, 32–34
Crucible, The, 32

F

fairy tales, 12, 37
familiars, 4, 12–14, 18
film, 4, 38–40

H

Harry Potter series, 35–37
Hartford witch panic, 24–26
His Dark Materials, 35

L

literature, 4, 32–37
Little Mermaid, The, 40

M

Macbeth, 11, 32

Mather, Increase, 19–21
Merlin, 37
myths, 6

P

Puritans, 15–17, 24, 37

R

runes, 11

S

Salem witch trials, 15–23
shape-shifting, 12, 14, 37
Sherwood, Grace, 27
"Sleeping Beauty," 12
"Snow White," 12
spectral evidence, 19–21
superstitions, 8–9

T

television, 37, 38
Tituba, 17

W

wands, 4, 6, 10, 11, 37
water test, 26, 27
white magic, 6, 9, 27
Wicca, 9

About the Author

J. Elizabeth Mills is a novel editor, as well as a writer. She lives in Seattle, Washington, and writes nonfiction books for children and teens.

Photo Credits

Cover, p. 1 © www.istockphoto.com/Fernando Gregory Milan; cover, p. 1 (background) alsamua/Shutterstock.com; pp. 3, 6, 15, 24 © www.istockpphoto.com/kycstudio; pp. 5, 16 The Bridgeman Art Library/Getty Images; p. 7 © Charles Walker/Topham/The Image Works; p. 8 Jason Hosking/Photographer's Choice/Getty Images; p. 10 Superstock/Getty Images; p. 13 Private Collection/Archives Charmet/The Bridgeman Art Library; p. 18 © Mary Evans Picture Library/The Image Works; p. 20 Stock Montage/Getty Images; p. 22 © North Wind Picture Archives via AP Images; p. 25 Peter Newark American Pictures/The Bridgeman Art Library; p. 28 Courtesy Robert G. Cunningham/totalsculptor.com; p. 30 © Bo Adams; p. 33 Photos.com/Thinkstock; p. 34 © AF archive/Alamy; p. 36 © Warner Bros. Pictures/Topham/The Image Works; p. 39 Virgil Apger/John Kobal Foundation/Getty Images; interior design elements © www.istockphoto.com/Dusko Jovic.

Designer: Nicole Russo; Editor: Bethany Bryan;
Photo Researcher: Amy Feinberg